THE PRINCIPLES OF STOCK MARKET

A Beginner's Guide for Wealth Creation.

COLLINS B. MORGAN

TABLE OF CONTENTS:

INTRODUCTION

This book delves into the intricacies of stock market investing, providing readers with a comprehensive roadmap and a guide to navigate the dynamic world of stocks. From understanding market fundamentals to implementing advanced investment strategies, this guide offers actionable insights for both novice and experienced investors.

Learn to analyze stocks, build a diversified portfolio, manage risks effectively, and develop a disciplined mindset for long-term success. With real-world examples and practical tips, **"The Principles of Stock Market"** equips readers with the knowledge and confidence to make informed investment decisions, ultimately paving the way to financial prosperity. Whether you're a beginner seeking a solid foundation or a seasoned investor looking to refine your approach, this book is your key guide to unlocking the full potential of the stock market.

CHAPTER ONE:

HISTORY OF STOCK MARKET AND ITS PURPOSES

The stock market, also known as the equity market, is a marketplace for buying and selling company stocks and other securities. It has a long and varied history, dating back to ancient civilizations such as the Romans and Greeks. However, the modern stock market can trace its roots to the 17th century when the first stock exchange was established in Amsterdam. Over the centuries, the stock market has undergone many changes, influenced by economic, political, and technological developments. The early stock market was not as organized or regulated as it is today. Trading was done in coffee houses and various other locations, and it was done mostly through informal agreements and hand-written contracts. The first formal stock exchange was created in Amsterdam in 1611, known as the Amsterdam Stock Exchange. It was established to facilitate trade in the securities of the Dutch East India Company, which was the world's first publicly traded company that issued stock. The success of the Amsterdam Stock Exchange led to the establishment of several other stock exchanges in Europe, including the London Stock Exchange in 1698 and the Paris Bourse in 1720. In the 18th and 19th centuries, the stock market played a crucial role in financing the growth of the industrial revolution. Companies like the East India Company and the Dutch East India Company expanded their businesses by selling shares to investors. This allowed for the development of large corporations and the accumulation of capital, leading to increased economic growth and prosperity. However, the stock market was also subject to speculative bubbles and crashes during this time, with the most famous being the South Sea Bubble in England and the Mississippi Bubble in France. The 20th century saw significant advancements in the stock market, with the introduction of electronic trading in the 1970s. This allowed for faster and more efficient trading, making the stock market more accessible to a wider range of investors. The creation of stock market indices, such as the Dow Jones Industrial Average, also helped investors track the overall performance of the market. The stock market has endured several significant events throughout its history, including the

Great Depression of 1929, which led to the creation of the Securities and Exchange Commission (SEC) in the United States to regulate the market and protect investors. In recent years, the stock market has also been influenced by technological advances, including the rise of online trading and high-frequency trading. These developments have increased the speed and complexity of trading, making the stock market more volatile and unpredictable. Today, the stock market is a vital part of the global economy, with billions of dollars traded daily. It plays a crucial role in financing businesses of all sizes, from small startups to large multinational corporations. The stock market is also a key indicator of the health of the economy, with fluctuations in stock prices often reflecting changes in economic conditions. In conclusion, the history of the stock market is a story of evolution and adaptation. From its humble beginnings in the 17th century to its current state as a complex and dynamic marketplace, the stock market has continuously evolved and continues to play a crucial role in the purpose of stock marketing and also to facilitate the buying and selling of stocks, which are shares of ownership in a company. It provides a platform for businesses to raise capital by selling shares to investors, and for investors to buy and sell shares for potential profits. Additionally, stock marketing allows for the efficient allocation of capital by directing investment towards companies with growth potential. It also serves as a barometerg for the overall health of the economy, as stock prices are influenced by various economic factors. Stock marketing also provides a means for individuals to save and invest for the future, as owning stocks can lead to potential long-term growth in wealth. It also allows for diversification of investments, as individuals can invest in a variety of companies across different industries and geographies. Overall, the purpose of stock marketing is to promote economic growth, provide opportunities for investment and savings, and facilitate the functioning of capital markets.

The stock market is a financial market where shares of publicly held companies are bought and sold. It provides a platform for companies to raise funds by selling ownership stakes to investors, and for investors to potentially profit from the increase in value of these company shares. Investing in the stock market involves buying shares of a company in the hope that the company will perform well and the value of the shares will increase. This can result in potential gains from selling the shares at a higher price, or from receiving dividends (a portion of the company's profits) paid out to shareholders. The performance of stock markets is influenced by a variety of factors including economic conditions, company performance, news and events, and investor sentiment. Changes in these factors can cause prices of stocks to fluctuate, which in turn affects the overall value of the stock market. Stock markets can be volatile, meaning prices can change quickly and significantly. This is because the buying and selling of stocks is determined by supply and demand from investors, which can be influenced by a wide range of factors. Different types of stock markets include the New York Stock Exchange and the Nasdaq in the United States, or the London Stock Exchange and Tokyo Stock Exchange in other countries. These markets have specific rules and regulations that govern the buying and selling of shares. Individuals can invest in the stock market through various methods, such as buying stocks directly, investing in a mutual fund or an exchange-traded fund (ETF), or using a robo-advisor or financial advisor. It is important to research and understand the risks and potential rewards before investing in the stock market. Diversifying investments across different types of stocks and industries can also help mitigate risk. Overall, the stock market plays an important role in the economy by providing a means for companies to raise capital and for individuals to invest and potentially grow their wealth. However, as with any investment, there are risks involved and it is important to carefully consider one's financial goals and risk tolerance before entering the stock market.

KEY PLAYERS IN STOCK MARKET

1. **Retail investors**: These are individual investors who buy and sell stocks for their personal investment portfolio. They usually trade through discount brokerages and online platforms.

2. **Institutional investors**: These are large financial institutions such as banks, insurance companies, pension funds, and hedge funds. They have significant capital and greater access to information and resources, allowing them to make large and strategic trades in the stock market.

3. **Stockbrokers**: Stockbrokers are licensed individuals or firms who act as intermediaries between buyers and sellers of stocks. They assist retail and institutional investors in buying and selling stocks in the stock market.

4. **Market Makers**: These are firms or individuals who facilitate the buying and selling of stocks by providing liquidity to the market. They do this by buying and holding stocks in large quantities and then selling them to other investors at a slightly higher price.

5. **Investment Banks**: Investment banks are financial institutions that help companies raise capital by issuing stocks and other

securities to the public. They also offer services such as underwriting, mergers and acquisitions, and financial advisory.

6. **Day traders**: Day traders are individuals who buy and sell stocks multiple times a day, trying to make small profits from price fluctuations. They usually use technical analysis and short-term strategies to make trading decisions.

7. **Stock Analysts**: These are professionals who study companies, industries, and the economy to provide insights and recommendations on stocks. They work for investment banks, financial institutions, and independent research firms.

8. **Financial Advisors**: Financial advisors are professionals who help investors create and manage their investment portfolios. They offer personalized advice on which stocks to buy and sell based on the investors' financial goals, risk tolerance, and investment horizon.

9. **Speculators**: Speculators are individuals who make high-risk, high-reward bets on stocks with the expectation of making a profit from short-term price fluctuations. They usually use leverage and often have a shorter investment horizon than traditional investors.

10. **Algorithmic traders**: These are traders who use computer programs and algorithms to automate trading decisions. They rely on mathematical models and data analysis to identify and execute trades at high speeds.

11. **Insider traders**: Insider traders are individuals who have access to non-public information about a company and use it to make profits by trading in its stock. This practice is illegal and can result in severe penalties.

12. **Foreign investors**: These are investors from other countries who trade in the stock market. They can be individuals or institutional investors seeking to diversify their portfolio or take advantage of opportunities in different markets.

13. **Short-sellers**: Short-sellers are investors who borrow shares from a broker and sell them, hoping to buy them back at a lower price in the future. They profit from the difference in the selling and buying price but also face the risk of unlimited losses if the stock price increases.

14. **Market regulators**: These are government agencies responsible for overseeing and regulating the stock market. They enforce rules

and regulations to ensure fair and transparent trading practices and protect investors' interests.

15. High-frequency traders: High-frequency traders use advanced technology and powerful computers to execute thousands of trades in a fraction of a second. They take advantage of small price discrepancies and make profits from high trading volumes.

16. Primary market investors: Primary market investors participate in the initial sale of stocks by a company through an initial public offering (IPO). They can be retail or institutional investors looking to buy shares of a newly listed company.

17. Secondary market investors: Secondary market investors buy and sell stocks on the secondary market, where stocks are actively traded after the IPO. It includes all the players mentioned above, except for primary market investors.

18. Mutual fund and ETF investors: These are investors who buy shares of mutual funds or exchange-traded funds (ETFs) that invPurpose of stock marketing
The purpose of stock marketing is to facilitate the buying and selling of stocks, which are shares of ownership in a company. It provides a platform for businesses to raise capital by selling shares

to investors, and for investors to buy and sell shares for potential profits.

l health of the economy, as stock prices

KNOWING HOW THE STOCK MARKET FUNCTIONS

The stock market is a place where shares of publicly traded companies are bought and sold. These shares represent ownership in a company and give investors the opportunity to profit from the company's success. Stock markets are typically organized into exchanges, such as the New York Stock Exchange (NYSE) or the Nasdaq. These exchanges provide a centralized location for buyers and sellers to meet and trade shares. The price of a stock is determined by the forces of supply and demand. If there are more buyers than sellers, the stock price will increase, and vice versa. This is why stock prices can fluctuate daily. Trading on the stock market is facilitated by intermediaries such as stockbrokers, who act as agents for investors, and market makers, who provide liquidity by buying and selling shares. Investors can buy and sell stocks through these intermediaries or through online trading platforms. The stock market is also influenced by various factors such as economic conditions, company performance, and news events. Investors often use fundamental and technical analysis to evaluate a company's financial health and determine a stock's potential value. Investing in the stock market comes with certain risks, as the value of stocks can go up or down. It is important for investors to diversify their portfolio and stay informed about the companies they invest in. The stock market can offer potential for long-term growth and can help individuals build wealth over time.

CHAPTER TWO

GETTING STARTED IN STOCK

Before getting started in stock marketing investment one needs to carefully follow this outlined steps one at a time. You have to;

1. Educate yourself Before jumping into stock market investing, it is important to educate yourself about the market and how it works. Read books, attend seminars, and do research online to gain a basic understanding of investing, stock market trends, and different investment strategies.

2. Consider and weigh your investment goals and risk tolerance Before investing in the stock market, it is important to have a clear idea of your investment goals and risk tolerance. Do you want long-term growth or short-term gains? How much loss can you afford to take? Knowing your goals and risk tolerance will help guide your investment decisions.

3. Choose a brokerage account To buy and sell stocks, you will need to open a brokerage account. There are many reputable online brokers that offer low fees and easy-to-use platforms. Take the time to research and compare different brokerage options to find the one that best suits your needs.

4. Start with a small amount It is always wise to start small when you are new to the stock market. Begin with a small amount of

money that you are comfortable risking and use it to get familiar with the process of buying and selling stocks.

5. Diversify your portfolio, One of the primary principles of successful investing is diversification. This means spreading your investments across different sectors and companies, rather than putting all your money into one stock. Diversification helps minimize risk and protect against losses.

6. Do your research Before investing in a company, make sure to do your due diligence. Research the company's financials, management team, products or services, and any potential risks. This will help you make correct investment decisions.

7. Monitor your investments Keep track of the performance of your investments and regularly review your portfolio. This will help you make necessary adjustments and re-balance your portfolio if needed.

8. Stay calm during market fluctuations The stock market can be unpredictable and there will inevitably be ups and downs. It is important to stay calm and resist the urge to make impulsive decisions during market fluctuations. Remember to focus on your long-term goals and avoid making emotional investment decisions.

9. Consider investing in index funds If you are new to stock market investing, consider investing in low-cost index funds. These funds track the performance of a market index, such as the S&P 500, and offer instant diversification with minimal risk.

10. Seek professional advice If you are unsure about how to get started in the stock market, or if you want a more personalized approach, consider seeking advice from a financial advisor. They can help you develop an investment strategy that aligns with your goals and risk tolerance.

SETTING INVESTMENT GOALS WITH STRATEGIES IN WINNING AND OBTAINING THEM

Setting investment objectives in stock marketing are essential in stock marketing as they provide a clear direction and focus for your investment decisions. They serve as a roadmap to help you achieve your financial goals and maximize your returns. Here are some key steps to set your investment objectives and goals in stock marketing:

1. **Determine your risk tolerance**: Before setting your investment goals, it's important to understand how much risk you are comfortable taking. This will help you select the right mix of investments that align with your risk tolerance.

2. **Identify your financial goals**: Think about what you want to achieve financially in the short-term and long-term. It could be saving for retirement, buying a house, or funding your child's education. Your financial goals will determine your investment objectives and timeframe.

3. Consider your time horizon: Your time horizon is the amount of time you have to reach your financial goals. If you have a longer time horizon, you may be able to take more risks and invest in more aggressive stocks. If your time horizon is shorter, you may want to focus on safer, less volatile investments.

4. Determine your asset allocation: Your asset allocation refers to the mix of stocks, bonds, and cash in your portfolio. It should be based on your risk tolerance, financial goals, and time horizon. Generally, a younger investor with a longer time horizon may have a higher allocation of stocks, while an older investor with a shorter time horizon may have a higher allocation of bonds.

5. Set specific and measurable goals: Your investment objectives and goals should be specific and measurable. For example, instead of saying "I want to make money in the stock market," set a specific goal such as "I want to earn a 10% annual return on my investment portfolio."

6. Be realistic: While it's important to set ambitious goals, it's also important to be realistic. Consider your risk tolerance and the current market conditions when setting your goals. It's better to have achievable goals that you can reach consistently rather than setting unrealistic goals and being disappointed when you don't achieve them.

7. Review and adjust regularly: Your investment objectives and goals may change over time, so it's important to review and adjust them regularly. Factors such as changes in your financial situation, market conditions, and risk tolerance may impact your goals and objectives. Regularly evaluating and adjusting your goals will help ensure that they remain relevant and achievable. In summary, setting investment objectives and goals is crucial for success in stock marketing. By considering your risk tolerance, financial goals, time horizon, and regularly reviewing and adjusting your goals, you can create a solid investment plan that aligns with your needs and helps you achieve your financial goals. Consider working with a financial advisor to help you develop a personalized investment strategy that fits your specific goals and objectives.

CHAPTER THREE

BUILDING A STRONG PORTFOLIO IN STOCK MARKETING

There are many different strategies that can be used to create a good investment portfolio in the stock market, so it's important to find the one that works best for your individual goals and risk tolerance. However, here is a sample portfolio that includes a mix of different types of stocks and a diversified approach to minimize risk.

1. **Large-cap stocks**: These are big, well-established companies with a market capitalization of over $10 billion. They tend to be less volatile than smaller companies and provide steady long-term growth. Some examples include: - Apple Inc. (AAPL) - Microsoft Corporation (MSFT) - Johnson & Johnson (JNJ)

2. **Growth stocks**: These are companies that are expected to have high earnings growth in the future. While they may be riskier, they also have the potential for greater returns. Some examples include: - Amazon.com Inc. (AMZN) - Netflix Inc. (NFLX) - Alphabet Inc. (GOOGL)

3. **Dividend-paying stocks**: These are stocks that regularly distribute a portion of their profits as dividends to shareholders. They can provide a steady stream of income and are less affected by

market volatility. Some examples include: - AT&T Inc. (T) - Coca-Cola Company (KO) - Procter & Gamble Co. (PG)

4. Emerging market stocks: These are stocks of companies based in developing countries with high growth potential. While these investments carry higher risks, they also offer the opportunity for significant returns. Some examples include: - Baidu Inc. (BIDU) - Alibaba Group Holding Ltd. (BABA) - MercadoLibre Inc. (MELI)

5. Index funds: These are pre-packaged portfolios that track a specific market index, such as the S&P 500 or Dow Jones Industrial Average. They offer a diversified approach and lower fees compared to actively managed funds. Some examples include: - Vanguard S&P 500 ETF (VOO).

6. Defensive stocks: These are stocks of companies that are less affected by economic downturns and can help protect against market volatility. Some examples include: - Wal-Mart Stores Inc. (WMT) - McDonald's Corporation (MCD) - Clorox Company (CLX) It's important to regularly revisit and rebalance your portfolio to ensure that it remains aligned with your investment goals and also seek a financial advisor before making any investment decisions.

SUCCESS INVESTMENT STRATEGIES:

WAYS TO CREATE A WELL ROUNDED PORTFOLIO IN STOCK MARKETING

A -rounded stock portfolio is a key component of a successful investment strategy, encompassing a diverse mix of assets to manage risk and maximize returns. Diversification is the cornerstone, spreading investments across various sectors, industries, and geographic regions. This mitigates the impact of poor performance in one area and enhances the potential for overall growth.

Start with blue-chip stocks, representing stable and established companies with a history of consistent dividends and steady growth. These serve as a reliable foundation for your portfolio. High-growth stocks, on the other hand, offer the potential for substantial returns but come with increased volatility. Balancing both ensures stability and growth opportunities.

Incorporating dividend-paying stocks provides a regular income stream, fostering financial stability. Dividends not only offer a source of passive income but also indicate a company's financial health and commitment to shareholders. Additionally, consider growth-oriented stocks, emphasizing companies with innovative products or services and strong potential for future expansion.

Including international stocks diversifies your portfolio geographically, reducing risk associated with any single country's economic performance. Exchange-traded funds (ETFs) tracking global indices or specific sectors offer an efficient way to achieve this diversification. Emerging markets, though riskier, can provide substantial growth opportunities.

In times of economic uncertainty, defensive stocks such as utilities, healthcare, and consumer staples often outperform. These sectors are less sensitive to economic downturns, acting as a hedge against market volatility. Conversely, cyclical stocks tied to economic cycles can offer growth potential during periods of expansion.

Allocate a portion of your portfolio to bonds, enhancing stability. Bonds provide fixed income and act as a counterbalance to the volatility of stocks. Government bonds are considered safer, while corporate bonds offer higher yields but come with increased risk. Adjust the bond-to-stock ratio based on your risk tolerance and investment goals.

Regularly rebalance your portfolio to maintain the desired asset allocation. Market conditions and individual investments evolve, impacting the original balance. Periodically reassess your risk tolerance, financial goals, and market trends to make informed adjustments. A disciplined, long-term approach is crucial for sustained success in the dynamic world of stock investing and always remember to follow this practical guide and strategies:

1. Diversify across industries and sectors: A well-rounded stock portfolio should not be heavily concentrated in one industry or sector. Instead, it should have a good mix of stocks from various sectors such as technology, healthcare, consumer goods, finance, etc. This diversification helps to reduce risk and protect against market volatility.

2. Invest in both large-cap and small-cap stocks: Large-cap stocks are typically stable, well-established companies with a solid track record, while small-cap stocks offer higher potential for growth. By investing in both, you can balance out potential gains and risks.

3. Consider international stocks: Expanding your portfolio to include international stocks can provide exposure to diverse economies and industries. This can help mitigate risks associated with any downturns in the domestic market.

4. Invest in different asset classes: Along with stocks, consider diversifying your portfolio with other asset classes like bonds, real estate investment trusts (REITs), and commodities. This can provide a hedge against market volatility and offer different sources of income and potential gains. **5. Include dividend-paying stocks**: Dividend-paying stocks can provide a steady stream of income, even during market downturns. Look for companies with a solid track record of paying dividends and a history of increasing them over time.

6. Research and choose individual stocks wisely: Instead of blindly following the recommendations of others, do your own research and choose stocks that align with your investment goals and risk tolerance. Consider factors such as company financials, management team, competitive advantage, and industry trends.

7. Plan for both short-term and long-term investments: A well-rounded portfolio should have a mix of short-term and long-term investments. Short-term investments can help provide liquidity and growing returns, while long-term investments can offer stability and growth over time.

8. Rebalance regularly: As market conditions change, your portfolio may become unbalanced. It's important to regularly review and rebalance your portfolio to maintain your desired asset allocation and risk tolerance.

9. Consider index funds and ETFs: Instead of investing in individual stocks, you can also diversify your portfolio with index funds and exchange-traded funds (ETFs). These funds track the performance of a specific index or sector and can offer a low-cost way to diversify your portfolio.

10. Stay informed and be patient: Keeping yourself informed about the market and your investments is crucial for maintaining a well-rounded portfolio. However, it's also important to be patient and not make impulsive decisions based on short-term market fluctuations. Remember to focus on your long-term investment goals and stick to your investment strategy.

TYPES OF INVESTMENT YOU NEED TO KNOW IN STOCK MARKETING

For you to be in the world of stock marketing you need to get yourself acquainted with these terminologies which will set you on the edge while discussing with your clients; and they are as follows:

1. **Stocks**: Investing in individual company stocks is a common type of investment in the stock market. Investors purchase a share of ownership in a company and can gain profits through stock price appreciation or dividends.

2. **Index Funds**: Index funds are a type of mutual fund that tracks a specific stock market index, such as the S&P 500. This type of investment offers diversification and lower risk compared to investing in individual stocks.

3. **Exchange-Traded Funds (ETFs):** ETFs are similar to index funds, but they can be traded like stocks. They offer diversification and lower fees compared to mutual funds.

4. **Bonds**: Bonds are a type of fixed-income investment that involves lending money to a corporation or government entity.

Investors receive regular interest payments and their principal investment back at maturity.

5. **Mutual Funds**: A mutual fund is a type of investment that pools money from multiple investors to purchase a diversified portfolio of securities, such as stocks, bonds, and ETFs.

6. **Options**: Options are financial derivatives that give an investor the right, but not the obligation, to buy or sell a security at a predetermined price within a specific time frame.

7. **Cryptocurrencies**: Cryptocurrencies such as Bitcoin and Ethereum have become popular investment options in recent years. They are decentralized digital currencies that are not backed by any government or central authority.

8. **Real Estate Investment Trusts (REITs)**: REITs allow investors to own a share of income-generating real estate properties, such as shopping malls, apartment complexes, and office buildings.

9. **Commodity Futures**: Commodity futures involve buying or selling a contract for a specific amount of a commodity, such as gold or oil, at a predetermined price in the future.

10. Certificates of Deposit (CDs): CDs are a type of savings account offered by banks that offer a **fixed** interest rate for a set period of time. They are considered a relatively low-risk investment option.

CONCEPT OF ASSETS ALLOCATION

Balancing Investments to Match Risk Tolerance In Stock

Asset allocation is the process of dividing an investment portfolio among different asset categories, such as stocks, bonds, cash, and real estate, in order to achieve a desired risk and return profile. It is an important investment strategy that allows investors to manage risk and optimize returns. There are three main asset classes: stocks, bonds, and cash. Stocks offer the potential for high returns but also come with a higher level of risk. Bonds offer a lower return potential but are considered less risky than stocks. Cash investments, such as savings accounts and certificates of deposit (CDs), have the lowest risk but also offer the lowest potential returns. Balancing investments across different asset classes is crucial in order to match risk tolerance. Risk tolerance refers to an individual's ability and willingness to take on risk in their investments. It is influenced by factors such as age, income, financial goals, and personal comfort level with volatility. Investors with a high risk tolerance may allocate a larger portion of their portfolio to stocks, as they are comfortable with the potential for higher returns, even if it comes with greater risk. On the other hand, investors with a low risk tolerance may allocate a larger portion of their portfolio to bonds and cash, in order to preserve capital and minimize the negative impact of market fluctuations. The key to effective asset allocation is to find the right balance between risk and return that aligns with an individual's risk tolerance and financial goals. This can be achieved by diversifying investments across different asset classes and rebalancing the portfolio regularly to maintain the desired asset allocation. It is important to note that asset allocation does not guarantee a profit or protect against loss in a down market. However, by diversifying investments, it can help mitigate risk and potentially increase returns over the long term. It is recommended to regularly review and adjust asset allocation as personal circumstances and market conditions change. Seeking advice from a financial advisor can also be helpful in determining an appropriate asset allocation strategy.

CHAPTER FOUR

METHODS IN ANALYZING AND RESEARCHING BEFORE INVESTMENT

How to Research and Analyze stocks before investment Investing in stocks can be a lucrative way to grow your wealth, but it also carries risks. Before making any investment decisions, it is important to research and analyze the stocks you are considering. Here are some steps to help you research and analyze stocks before investing:

1. **Understand the basics of stock investing**: Before diving into stock research, make sure you have a basic understanding of how the stock market works, the different types of stocks (such as common stocks and preferred stocks), and the risks involved in stock investing.

2. **Determine your investment goals and risk tolerance**: It's important to have a clear understanding of your investment goals – such as long-term growth or generating regular income – and your risk tolerance, which will help guide your stock selection.

3. **Research the company**: A good place to start is by researching the company whose stock you are interested in. Look at the company's financial reports, including its income statement, balance sheet, and cash flow statement, to get an understanding of its financial health.

4. Analyze the industry and market trends: It's important to also consider the industry the company operates in and the overall market trends. Is the industry growing or declining? Is the company well-positioned within its industry? What are the current and predicted market trends that may impact the company's performance?

5. Evaluate the company's management team: The management team plays a crucial role in the success of a company. Look into the background and experience of the company's CEO, CFO, and other key executives. Are they experienced and have a strong track record? Do they have a clear strategy for the company's growth?

6. Check the company's valuation: The stock price of a company should reflect its true value. It's important to compare the company's stock price to its earnings, revenues, and other financial metrics to determine if its stock is undervalued or overvalued.

7. Look at the company's competitive advantage: A company with a strong competitive advantage is more likely to succeed and generate returns for its investors. Look into what makes the company stand out from its competitors and if it has a sustainable competitive advantage.

8. Research the company's debt and cash flow: A company's financial health is also impacted by its debt and cash flow. Look at the company's debt levels and how it is managing its cash flow. A company with high levels of debt and poor cash flow management may be at risk.

9. Read analyst reports and news articles: Analyst reports and news articles can provide valuable insights into a company. Look at different viewpoints and opinions to get a well-rounded understanding of the company's performance and prospects.

10. Understand the company's dividend policy: If the company pays dividends, research its dividend history and future plans for dividends. A company with a consistent and growing dividend policy can be a good sign of a stable and profitable company.

11. Use stock analysis tools: There are many online tools and platforms that can help you analyze stocks, such as financial data websites, stock screeners, and stock analysis software. These tools can help you with in-depth analysis and comparison of stocks.

12. Consult with a financial advisor: If you are unsure about how to research and analyze stocks, it's always a good idea to consult with a financial advisor. They can provide personalized advice and help you make informed investment decisions. Remember, stock research and analysis is an ongoing process. It's important to regularly review your investments and stay updated on any news or developments that may impact the stocks you hold. By doing thorough research and analysis, you can make informed investment decisions and increase your chances of success in the stock market.

GUIDE ON DIFFERENT METHODS OF STOCK MARKETING ANALYSIS YOU NEED TO FOLLOW

Stock market analysis involves various methods to assess the performance and potential of stocks. Here's a comprehensive guide on different methods:

1. **Fundamental Analysis** - This method involves studying financial and economic data of a company to determine its intrinsic value and potential for growth.

2. **Technical Analysis** - This approach uses charts and historical price patterns to forecast the future price direction of a stock.

3. **Sentiment Analysis** - This involves analyzing investor sentiment, behavioral finance, and market psychology to predict how the market will react to a stock.

4. **Quantitative Analysis** - This method uses mathematical and statistical models to analyze stock data and identify potential patterns and trends.

5. **Inter-market Analysis** - This type of analysis involves studying the relationship between different markets, such as stocks, bonds, commodities, and currencies, to identify trends and correlations.

6. **Event-Driven Analysis** - This approach focuses on market-moving events, such as earnings releases, mergers and

acquisitions, or government policy changes, to assess the impact on a stock's performance.

7. Sector and Industry Analysis - This method involves analyzing the performance of a stock in relation to its industry and sector peers to identify potential opportunities and risks.

8. Trend Analysis - This involves analyzing a stock's price movement over a specified period to determine its long-term trend and potential future direction.

9. Valuation Analysis - This approach uses various valuation techniques, such as price-to-earnings ratio or discounted cash flow analysis, to determine the fair value of a stock.

10. Top-Down and Bottom-Up Analysis - These are two broad approaches to stock market analysis, where top-down analysis starts with the big picture of the economy and then narrows down to individual stocks, while bottom-up analysis starts with individual companies and then expands to the overall market.

GUIDE ON STRATEGIES ON BUYING AND SELLING STOCKS

Strategizing for buying and selling stocks involves careful planning, research, and control over your investments. Here are some steps and considerations to help guide your strategy:

1. **Set Your Investment Goals**: Before you start buying and selling stocks, it's important to define your investment goals. Consider factors such as your risk tolerance, investment horizon, and financial objectives. This will help you determine the types of stocks to invest in and the level of risk you are comfortable with.

 2. **Do Your Research**: It's crucial to thoroughly research the stocks you are interested in buying or selling. This involves analyzing the financial performance of the company, its market trends, and any external factors that may impact its stock price. You can use tools such as financial reports, analyst ratings, and news articles to gather information.

3. **Diversify Your Portfolio**: It's generally recommended to diversify your investments by investing in different industries, sectors, and stocks. This can help reduce your risk exposure and prevent losses if one stock underperforms.

4. **Develop a Trading Plan**: A trading plan outlines your buying and selling strategies and helps keep you disciplined in your decision-making process. It should include your investment goals, risk management strategies, and criteria for entering and exiting a trade.

5. **Monitor Market Trends**: Keeping an eye on market trends and conditions can help guide your buying and selling decisions. This includes monitoring economic indicators, company news, and sector performance.

6. Utilize Technical Analysis: Technical analysis involves studying stock price patterns and trends to make buying and selling decisions. This can help you identify potential entry and exit points for trades based on historical price movements.

7. Consider Fundamental Analysis: Fundamental analysis involves evaluating the financial health of a company to determine its intrinsic value. This can help you make informed decisions about when to buy or sell a stock based on its current and potential future value.

8. Use Stop Loss and Limit Orders: Stop loss and limit orders are risk management tools that can help you control your trades. A stop loss order sets a specific price at which a stock will be sold to limit potential losses, while a limit order sets the maximum and minimum prices at which a stock will be bought or sold.

9. Stay Disciplined: It's important to stick to your trading plan and not let emotions, like fear or greed, control your decisions. Staying disciplined can help you avoid impulsive and potentially costly trading decisions.

10. Continuously Evaluate and Adjust: As market conditions and trends change, it's important to continuously evaluate and adjust your trading strategy. This will help ensure that your investments align with your goals and risk tolerance. Remember, successful buying and selling of stocks requires patience, discipline, and continuous learning. No strategy guarantees success, so it's important to do your due diligence, seek professional advice when necessary, and always be prepared for the potential risks and rewards of investing in stocks.

RISK MANAGEMENTS

SETTING PRICE TARGETS

Setting price targets and using stop-loss orders are important strategies for managing risk in bond investing. Here are some reasons why:

1. **Helps to limit losses**: Price targets and stop-loss orders can help investors to limit their losses in case the bond's market price falls. By setting a price target, investors can determine at what price they want to sell the bond, which can help them avoid larger losses if the bond's price continues to decline. Likewise, a stop-loss order will trigger a sell order when the bond's price reaches a certain level, preventing further losses.

2. **Encourages disciplined investing**: Having a predetermined price target or stop-loss order in place helps investors to stay disciplined in their investing approach. It can prevent them from holding on to a bond for too long in hopes of a price recovery, which can lead to bigger losses.

3. **Allows for profit-taking**: Price targets can also be used to take profits when the bond's price reaches a certain level. This can help

investors to lock in gains and prevent them from being wiped out in case the bond's price falls in the future.

4. Helps to manage emotions: Bonds, like any other investment, can be subject to market volatility. Setting price targets and stop-loss orders can help investors to manage their emotions and avoid making impulsive decisions based on short-term market fluctuations.

5. Facilitates portfolio rebalancing: Price targets and stop-loss orders can also be useful for rebalancing a portfolio. If a bond's price has appreciated significantly, it may be a good time to sell and reinvest the profits into other investments. On the other hand, if a bond's price has fallen, a stop-loss order can help to prevent further losses and free up capital for other investment opportunities. In summary, setting price targets and using stop-loss orders are effective risk management strategies for bond investors. They can help to minimize losses, encourage disciplined investing, facilitate profit-taking, manage emotions, and facilitate portfolio rebalancing. Investors should carefully assess their risk tolerance and investment goals before implementing these strategies and regularly review and adjust them as needed.

CHAPTER FIVE

UNDERSTANDING MARKET TRENDS

The market trend in stock refers to the overall direction or movement of the stock market as a whole. It is influenced by various factors, both internal and external, that impact the buying and selling behavior of investors. One of the most significant influencers of the market trend in stock is the overall sentiment of the market, which is influenced by economic conditions and market news. Other key influencers of the market trend in stock include:

1. Macroeconomic factors: The overall state of the economy, including inflation, interest rates, and GDP growth, can greatly influence the market trend in stock. A healthy economy generally leads to a bullish trend in the stock market, while a struggling economy can result in a bearish trend.

2. Corporate earnings: The financial performance of companies, particularly large ones, can have a significant impact on the market trend in stock. Strong earnings reports from companies can boost investor confidence and drive the market trend upwards, while poor earnings reports can have the opposite effect.

3. Geopolitical events: Factors such as political instability, trade wars, and international conflicts can impact the market trend in stock. These events can create uncertainty and volatility in the stock market, leading to potential swings in the market trend.

4. **Market sentiment**: The overall mood or sentiment of investors can greatly influence the market trend in stock. If investors are optimistic about the market, it can lead to a bullish trend, while pessimism can result in a bearish trend.

5. **Technical analysis**: Traders and investors often use technical analysis to study historical price patterns and market trends to make decisions about buying and selling. The use of technical indicators and signals can also impact the market trend in stock.

6. **Monetary policies**: The actions and decisions of central banks, such as interest rate changes and quantitative easing, can also impact the market trend in stock. These policies can influence the availability of credit and the flow of money, which can have a direct effect on the stock market.

7. **Sector-specific trends**: Certain industries or sectors can experience different market trends based on their performance and outlook. For example, a bullish trend may be seen in the technology sector due to the growing demand for technology products and services. Overall, the market trend in stock is a reflection of the collective behavior and sentiment of market participants and is influenced by a wide range of factors. It is essential for investors to understand these influencers and closely monitor market trends to make informed decisions about their investments.

TECHNICAL ANALYSIS TOOLS IN MAKING DECISIONS

Technical analysis is a method that uses past price and volume data to identify patterns and predict future price movements of stocks. It is based on the assumption that market trends tend to repeat themselves and that history can provide insights into the future. In order to make decisions using technical analysis, investors use a variety of tools and indicators to analyze price charts and identify potential trading opportunities. Some common technical analysis tools include:

1. **Moving Averages**: Moving averages are used to identify trends and support/resistance levels in stock prices. They smooth out fluctuations and provide a visual representation of a stock's price trend.

2. **Support and Resistance Levels**: Support and resistance levels are price points that a stock struggles to move beyond, either upwards or downwards. These levels are typically determined by previous highs and lows in the stock's price history, and they can help investors identify potential entry or exit points.

3. **Relative Strength Index (RSI)**: The RSI is a momentum oscillator that measures the speed and change of price movements to determine if a stock is overbought or oversold. It is used to identify

potential entry or exit points based on the stock's current price momentum.

4. Bollinger Bands: Bollinger Bands are statistical charts that measure the volatility of a stock's price movements. They consist of three bands — an upper band, a lower band, and a middle band. When the price rises above or falls below the upper or lower band, it is considered to be a potential signal that the stock is overbought or oversold.

5. Candlestick Charts: Candlestick charts are a popular charting method that displays a stock's open, high, low, and closing prices for a given time period. They are useful in identifying price patterns and trends, and can help investors make decisions based on the direction of a stock's price movements.

6. Volume Analysis: Volume analysis is a method of analyzing the trading volume of a stock over time. High volume typically indicates strong buying or selling pressure, and can help investors predict future price movements. It is important to note that technical analysis tools are not foolproof and should not be solely relied upon for making investment decisions. Other factors such as fundamental analysis, market trends, and company news should also be taken into consideration. Additionally, technical analysis is not an exact science and requires a certain level of interpretation and understanding to be effectively used in decision-making.

CHAPTER SIX

MANAGING RISKS AND EMOTIONS

The stock market is a highly unpredictable and volatile environment, whereby investors have to constantly manage risks and emotions. Investing in stocks can bring significant returns, but it also carries a substantial amount of risk. As a result, it's important for investors to have a strong understanding of how to manage risks and emotions in stock marketing.

Managing Risks:

1. Educate Yourself:

First and foremost, it's crucial for investors to educate themselves about the stock market and the different types of risks associated with it. This includes understanding how the market works, the various investment options available, and the types of risks that can impact stock prices.

2. Diversify Your Portfolio:

One of the key ways to manage risk in the stock market is to diversify your portfolio. This means investing in a variety of stocks from different industries and sectors, rather than putting all your eggs in one basket. Diversifying your portfolio helps to minimize the impact of market fluctuations and reduces the risk of losing all your investments.

3. Set Realistic Goals:

Having realistic expectations and goals when investing in the stock market is essential in managing risks. Setting realistic goals also helps to avoid making impulsive and emotional decisions.

4. Regularly Monitor Your Investments:

It's important for investors to regularly monitor their investments and stay up to date on market trends and news. This will help them to make informed decisions and identify potential risks that may arise.

Emotional Management:

1. Keep Emotions in Check:

A common mistake made by investors is letting emotions drive their investment decisions. Emotions such as fear, greed, and overconfidence can lead to impulsive and irrational decisions, which can result in significant losses. It's important for investors to keep their emotions in check and make logical and informed decisions based on research and analysis.

2. Stick to Your Plan:

Having a solid investment plan in place can help investors to stay grounded and avoid making emotional decisions. This will prevent you from making hasty decisions that could negatively impact your investments.

3. Avoid Following the Herd:

Following the crowd and investing based on market trends and hype can be a dangerous strategy. It's important for investors to do their own research and make their own decisions rather than being influenced by others. This will prevent them from making impulsive decisions based on emotions.

4. Learn from Your Mistakes:

Investing in the stock market is a continuous learning process, and it's inevitable that investors will make mistakes along the way. Instead of dwelling on these mistakes, it's important to learn from them and use them as a way to improve your investment strategies in the future.

In conclusion, managing risks and emotions is crucial in stock marketing to ensure long-term success and profitability. By educating yourself, diversifying your portfolio, setting realistic goals, and managing emotions, investors can minimize risks and make well-informed decisions that will lead to a successful investment journey. It's also important to remember that investing in the stock market carries a certain level of risk, and it's essential to have a long-term perspective and trust the process.

CHAPTER SEVEN

ROLES OF TAX IN STOCK MARKETING

Taxes play an important role in the stock market, as they can significantly impact the profitability of investments and the behavior of market participants. In this guide, we will discuss the various roles of taxes in the stock market and how they affect investors and businesses.

1. Capital gains taxes

Capital gains taxes are taxes levied on the profits made from selling a stock at a higher price than it was bought. These taxes are a major source of government revenue and are an essential part of the tax system in most countries.

Investors are required to pay taxes on capital gains when they sell stocks, and the tax rate can vary depending on the holding period of the investment. Short-term capital gains, meaning gains from stocks held for less than a year, are usually taxed at a higher rate than long-term gains.

The impact of capital gains taxes on the stock market is significant, as it can affect the behavior of investors. For example, investors may be more inclined to hold onto their investments for longer periods to take advantage of lower tax rates on long-term gains. This can lead to a decrease in trading activity in the market, which can affect the liquidity and volatility of stocks.

2. Dividend taxes

Dividends are one of the primary ways in which companies distribute profits to their shareholders. These payouts are subject to dividend taxes, which are a form of income tax on the earnings received from stocks.

The tax rate for dividends can also vary depending on the holding period of the stock. Dividends received from stocks held for a shorter period may be taxed at a higher rate, while dividends from long-term holdings may be taxed at a lower rate. This is known as the qualified dividend rate, which is usually lower than the ordinary income tax rate.

The taxation of dividends can have a significant impact on the income of investors, especially those who rely on dividends as a source of regular income. It can also affect a company's decision to distribute dividends, as higher tax rates can make it less attractive for companies to pay out dividends to their shareholders.

3. Corporate taxes

Corporate taxes are an essential source of government revenue and play a significant role in the stock market. These taxes are levied on the profits of companies and can vary depending on the country and the industry in which the company operates.

When a company pays a higher tax rate on its profits, it can reduce the amount of money available for reinvestment and distribution to its shareholders. This can affect the stock's performance and the confidence of investors in the company's future growth prospects.

4. Taxes on specific types of investments

Aside from capital gains and dividend taxes, there are also specific taxes on certain types of investments, such as options and futures trades. For example, in the United States, options trades are subject to a tax known as the Options Regulatory Fee (ORF), which is used to cover the costs of regulating and overseeing options trading on national exchanges.

These types of taxes can affect the trading activity of these specific investments and may also impact the risk-reward profiles of these trades for investors.

5. Effects on market participation and behavior

Taxes can influence the behavior of market participants, including individual and institutional investors. High tax rates on capital gains and dividends may discourage individuals from actively participating in the stock market, while lower tax rates may encourage more trading activity.

Institutional investors, such as hedge funds and mutual funds, may also consider the tax implications of their investment decisions, as they seek to maximize returns for their investors.

6. Government policies and the stock market

Tax policies and changes in tax rates can have a significant impact on the stock market. When governments introduce new tax policies or propose changes to existing ones, it can cause market volatility and affect investor sentiment.

For example, proposed cuts to corporate tax rates may boost stock prices and the overall market, as companies are likely to have more money for reinvestment and growth. On the other hand, increases in capital gains or dividend taxes may have a negative impact on the stock market, as investors may expect to receive lower returns on their investments, Taxes play several important roles in the stock market, from generating government revenue to influencing the behavior of market participants. Investors and businesses must consider the impact of taxes on their investments and strategies, as they can significantly affect the profitability and performance of the stock market. Staying informed about tax policies and changes is crucial for making informed investment decisions.

In conclusion, the world of stock marketing is a complex and ever-evolving landscape that requires in-depth knowledge and understanding to navigate successfully. Whether you are a beginner aiming to enter the market or a seasoned investor looking to improve your skills, there is a wealth of information and resources available in the form of stock marketing books. These books cover a wide range of topics, from fundamental analysis and technical analysis to trading strategies and risk management. They are written by experienced professionals and experts in the field, providing readers with valuable insights, tips, and techniques to help them maximize their profits and minimize their losses. One of the key takeaways from stock marketing books is the importance of research and analysis. In order to make sound investment decisions, it is essential to have a thorough understanding of the market, the economy, and the companies you are interested in. This can be achieved through techniques such as fundamental analysis, which involves evaluating a company's financial health, management team, and market positioning, and technical analysis, which involves studying patterns and trends in stock prices. Stock marketing books also emphasize the significance of having a solid investment strategy. This includes setting clear objectives, developing a diversified portfolio, and implementing risk management techniques. A well-defined strategy can provide investors with a disciplined and structured approach to decision-making, helping them stay focused and avoid impulsive or emotional trading. Moreover, these books shed light on the various factors that impact the stock market, such as economic indicators, political events, and global trends. They also discuss the different types of stocks and investment assets, such as stocks, bonds, mutual funds, and options, and provide insights into their potential risks and rewards. In addition to the technical aspects of stock marketing, these books also touch upon the psychological aspects and the role of emotions in investing. They highlight the importance of maintaining a rational and disciplined mindset, and avoiding common pitfalls such as greed and fear, which can often lead to irrational decision-making and financial losses. Furthermore, stock marketing books offer a glimpse into the history of the stock market, its evolution, and major events that have shaped it. This helps readers gain a better understanding of market cycles and trends, and learn from past mistakes and successes. Overall, stock marketing books offer a comprehensive and in-depth guide to the world of investing. They provide readers with valuable tools, knowledge, and strategies that can help them navigate the market and make informed decisions. However, it is important to note that these books cannot predict market movements or guarantee success. Market conditions are always subject to change, and it is important for investors to continuously educate themselves and adapt their strategies accordingly. In conclusion, stock marketing books are an invaluable resource for anyone looking to enter or improve their skills in the stock market. They offer a wealth of information, insights, and advice that can be crucial in achieving long-term success in this complex and dynamic field. With the right knowledge and strategy, investors can harness the power of the stock market to grow and protect their wealth.

IMPACTS OF TECHNOLOGICAL ADVANCES IN STOCK MARKETING

Technological advances have significantly transformed the landscape of stock markets, impacting various aspects from trading practices to market efficiency. One notable change is the advent of electronic trading platforms, which have replaced traditional floor trading and enabled faster, more efficient transactions. These platforms facilitate high-frequency trading, where algorithms execute numerous trades in fractions of a second, influencing market liquidity and volatility.

Moreover, the rise of big data and advanced analytics has empowered investors to make more informed decisions. Machine learning algorithms analyze vast datasets, identifying patterns and trends that might be imperceptible to human traders. This has led to the development of algorithmic trading strategies, further shaping market dynamics.

The proliferation of mobile applications and online brokerage platforms has democratized access to stock markets, allowing individual investors to participate more actively. This accessibility, coupled with real-time market information, has increased retail trading volumes and altered market sentiment.

Blockchain technology has introduced decentralized finance (DeFi) and cryptocurrencies, challenging traditional stock market structures. Smart contracts and tokenization offer new ways to trade and invest, reducing the reliance on intermediaries and enhancing transparency.

Despite these advancements, concerns about market integrity have arisen. Cybersecurity threats pose risks to electronic trading platforms, potentially leading to financial disruptions. The "flash crash" of 2010 highlighted the susceptibility of automated trading systems to unforeseen events, prompting ongoing discussions about market resilience and the need for regulatory frameworks to keep pace with technological evolution.

In conclusion, technological advances in stock markets have brought about profound changes, enhancing efficiency, accessibility, and analytical capabilities. However, they also present challenges, such as cybersecurity risks and the need for adaptive regulations. Striking a balance between innovation and stability is crucial for the continued evolution of the financial markets.

Technological advances have significantly impacted the stock market in various ways:

1. **Algorithmic Trading**:

- Automated trading algorithms execute high-frequency trades at speeds impossible for humans. This can enhance market liquidity but may also contribute to increased market volatility.

2. **Big Data and Analytics**:

   - The ability to process vast amounts of data has improved market analysis. Investors can make more informed decisions by leveraging data analytics for predictive modeling and risk management.

3. **High-Frequency Trading (HFT)**:

   - High-frequency traders use advanced algorithms to execute trades in milliseconds, taking advantage of small price discrepancies. While it enhances liquidity, critics argue it may lead to market inefficiencies.

4. **Blockchain and Cryptocurrencies**:

   - Cryptocurrencies play a significant role in the stock market by introducing new dimensions of investment and financial innovation. Unlike traditional stocks, cryptocurrencies operate on decentralized blockchain technology, providing several unique advantages. Firstly, they offer increased accessibility, allowing individuals worldwide to participate in the market without the barriers of traditional financial systems. This inclusivity has the potential to democratize finance and empower individuals who may not have had access to traditional stock markets.

Additionally, cryptocurrencies provide a hedge against inflation and economic uncertainties. With a fixed supply and decentralized nature, some view cryptocurrencies, especially Bitcoin, as a store of value similar to precious metals like gold. This perceived resilience to inflation can attract investors looking for alternative assets to diversify their portfolios and mitigate risks associated with traditional fiat currencies.

The technology underlying cryptocurrencies, blockchain, ensures transparency, security, and immutability of transactions. This can enhance trust in financial systems and reduce the risk of fraud, providing a level of accountability that traditional financial institutions may struggle to achieve. As a result, blockchain technology is being explored for various applications beyond cryptocurrencies, such as supply chain management, healthcare, and more.

Furthermore, the advent of decentralized finance (DeFi) built on blockchain platforms has disrupted traditional financial intermediaries. Decentralized exchanges, lending protocols, and other financial services offer users greater control over their assets, cutting out middlemen and potentially reducing transaction costs.

Despite these advantages, it's crucial to acknowledge the volatility and regulatory uncertainties associated with cryptocurrencies. The prices of cryptocurrencies can experience significant fluctuations, making them high-risk investments. Regulatory developments worldwide also impact the cryptocurrency market, creating both challenges and opportunities.

In conclusion, the importance of cryptocurrencies in the stock market lies in their potential to transform the financial landscape. They provide a decentralized and inclusive alternative, offering new investment opportunities and challenging traditional financial norms. However, the evolving nature of this market requires careful consideration of risks and a dynamic approach to regulation and technological advancements.

Technologies like blockchain underpin cryptocurrencies, introducing decentralized and secure transaction systems. This has led to the emergence of digital assets and alternative investment opportunities.

5. **Online Trading Platforms:**
   - User-friendly online platforms enable individual investors to trade stocks easily. This democratization of

access has increased market participation but also requires investors to be more tech-savvy.

6. Artificial Intelligence (AI):

- AI is used for market prediction, sentiment analysis, and algorithmic trading. It can process vast amounts of data to identify patterns and trends, aiding investors in making more informed decisions.

7. Robo-Advisors:

- Automated financial advisors use algorithms to provide investment advice and manage portfolios. This has made investment services more accessible, particularly for those with smaller portfolios.

8. Electronic Communication Networks (ECNs):

- ECNs facilitate direct trading between institutional investors, reducing the need for traditional intermediaries. This can result in faster and more efficient order execution.

9. Cybersecurity Challenges:

- The increased reliance on technology also brings cybersecurity risks. Hacking attempts and data breaches can impact market integrity and investor confidence.

10. Global Connectivity:

- Technology has made markets more interconnected globally. Events in one part of the world can quickly influence markets elsewhere, requiring investors to consider a broader range of factors.

While technological advances offer many benefits, they also pose challenges and require continuous monitoring and adaptation within the financial industry.

FOUR BASIC COMPONENT OF A STOCK:

Investing has a set of four basic elements that investors use to break down a stock's value. In this article, we will look at four commonly used financial ratios

- **price-to-book (P/B) ratio**

The Price-to-Book Ratio (P/B ratio) is a financial metric used to evaluate a company's market value relative to its book value. It is calculated by dividing the market price per share by the book value per share. The market price represents the current stock price, while the book value is the net asset value of the company per share, derived from its balance sheet.

A P/B ratio below 1 suggests that the market values the company lower than its book value, possibly indicating that the stock is undervalued. Investors may see this as an opportunity to buy shares at a discount. Conversely, a P/B ratio above 1 implies that the market values the company higher than its book value, suggesting the stock may be overvalued.

However, relying solely on the P/B ratio has limitations. It doesn't consider factors such as future growth potential, earnings, or the quality of assets. Industries with intangible assets, like technology or pharmaceuticals, might have higher P/B ratios due to the significant value of intellectual property not fully reflected in book value.

Furthermore, comparing P/B ratios across industries may be misleading, as different sectors have varying capital structures and asset characteristics. It's crucial to interpret the P/B ratio within the context of the specific industry and company dynamics.

In summary, while the P/B ratio is a valuable tool for assessing a stock's relative value, investors should complement it with a comprehensive analysis of other financial metrics and qualitative factors to make well-informed investment decisions.

- **price-to-earnings (P/E) ratio:**

The Price-to-Earnings (P/E) ratio is a fundamental financial metric used by investors to evaluate the relative value of a stock. It is calculated by dividing the current market price per share by the earnings per share (EPS) over the most recent 12-month period.

This ratio provides insights into how much investors are willing to pay for each dollar of earnings generated by a company.

A high P/E ratio may indicate that investors have high expectations for a company's future earnings growth, potentially making it an attractive investment. However, it could also suggest that the stock is overvalued. On the other hand, a low P/E ratio may signal undervaluation, but it could also reflect lower growth prospects or increased risk.

Investors often compare a company's P/E ratio to others in the same industry or sector to assess its relative valuation. A company with a lower P/E ratio than its peers might be considered a better value, assuming similar growth prospects and risk profiles.

It's crucial to consider the context when interpreting P/E ratios. For example, cyclical industries might have lower P/E ratios during economic downturns due to reduced earnings, but this doesn't necessarily mean the stocks are undervalued. Similarly, high-growth tech companies might have elevated P/E ratios because investors anticipate substantial future earnings.

However, P/E ratios have limitations. They don't account for differences in growth rates, risk, or quality of earnings. Additionally, companies with negative earnings or low earnings volatility may not be well-represented by P/E ratios.

In summary, while the P/E ratio is a valuable tool for assessing a stock's relative valuation, investors should use it in conjunction with other financial metrics and consider the broader economic and industry context for a comprehensive analysis.

- **price-to-earnings growth (PEG) ratio:**

Price-to-Earnings Growth (PEG) is a financial metric used by investors to evaluate the relationship between a stock's current price-to-earnings (P/E) ratio and its projected earnings growth rate. It provides a more comprehensive analysis than the P/E ratio alone, as it takes into account the company's earnings growth potential.

To calculate the PEG ratio, one typically divides the P/E ratio by the annual earnings growth rate. A PEG ratio below 1 is generally considered favorable, indicating that the stock may be undervalued relative to its earnings growth potential. Conversely, a PEG ratio above 1 may suggest that the stock is overvalued compared to its expected growth rate.

Investors value PEG ratio because it helps them assess not only a company's current valuation but also its growth prospects. A low PEG ratio might indicate that the market has not fully priced in the company's growth potential, presenting an opportunity for investors. However, it's essential to consider other factors like industry trends, economic conditions, and company-specific risks before making investment decisions.

It's important to note that PEG ratios have limitations. For instance, they rely on projected earnings growth, which can be uncertain. Additionally, different industries may have varying acceptable PEG ratios, as growth expectations differ.

In summary, the PEG ratio offers a nuanced perspective by combining the P/E ratio with expected earnings growth. Investors utilize this metric to identify potentially undervalued or overvalued stocks, though it's crucial to interpret it alongside other financial indicators and consider the broader market context.

- **Dividend yield:**

Dividend yield is a financial metric that indicates the annual dividend income an investor can expect to receive from an investment in a particular stock, expressed as a percentage of the stock's current market price. It is calculated by dividing the annual dividend per share by the current market price per share and multiplying the result by 100.

Investors often look at dividend yield as an important factor when evaluating potential investments, as it provides insight into the income-generating potential of a stock. A higher dividend yield may be attractive to income-seeking investors, such as those in retirement, who rely on regular dividend payments as a source of passive income.

However, a high dividend yield should not be viewed in isolation. It's crucial to consider the sustainability of the dividend. A company with a high dividend yield may not be a sound investment if its earnings and cash flow do not support the dividend payments. Therefore, analysts often assess the payout ratio, which compares the dividends paid to the company's earnings.

Furthermore, changes in stock prices can impact dividend yield. If a stock's price drops significantly, the dividend yield will increase, even if the company hasn't changed its dividend payments. Conversely, a rising stock price could result in a lower dividend yield.

Investors should also be aware of potential red flags, such as an unusually high dividend yield that may signal financial distress within the company or an imminent dividend cut. Understanding the company's financial health, business model, and industry trends is crucial for making informed decisions about investing based on dividend yield.

In summary, while dividend yield is a valuable metric for income-oriented investors, it should be considered alongside other factors, including the company's financial health, payout ratio, and overall market conditions, to make well-informed investment decisions.

GOLDEN RULES OF SAFE STOCK INVESTING

First Golden Rule: 'Buy what's worth owning forever'

This rule tells you that when you are selecting which stock to buy, you should think as if you will co-own the company forever. So before you decide to co-own a company, you need to study the company very carefully and find out whether it is really a wonderful business.

This is beautifully said by Warren Buffett; " **Our favorite holding period is forever** " and to avoid temptation about buying stocks which don't meet this criteria, he said " **If you don't feel comfortable owning a business for 10 years, then don't own it even for 10 minutes**".

Investing in the stock market is a nuanced endeavor that demands a comprehensive understanding of market dynamics, risk management, and financial analysis. In conclusion, the decision to invest in stocks should be underpinned by a strategic approach, informed decision-making, and a long-term perspective. It's essential for investors to conduct thorough research, diversify their portfolios, and remain resilient in the face of market volatility.

Moreover, successful stock market investing requires a disciplined mindset that withstands the temptations of short-term gains and emotional reactions to market fluctuations. Patience is a virtue in the realm of investing, allowing time for compounding returns to work in your favor. By adopting a patient approach, investors can weather market downturns and capitalize on the potential for long-term wealth accumulation.

Diversification is a key tenet of a robust investment strategy. Spreading investments across different sectors, industries, and asset classes can mitigate risk and enhance the overall stability of a portfolio. This not only safeguards against the underperformance of a specific stock or sector but also positions the investor to capitalize on opportunities that may arise in diverse market conditions.

Risk management is another critical aspect of successful investing. Understanding and quantifying risk, setting realistic expectations, and establishing clear financial goals contribute to a well-rounded risk management strategy. By having a clear understanding of one's risk tolerance, investors can make informed decisions and avoid succumbing to panic during turbulent market periods.

Continuous learning is imperative for anyone navigating the complexities of the stock market. Staying abreast of economic indicators, industry trends, and company fundamentals allows investors to make informed decisions based on a solid foundation of knowledge. Embracing a mindset of lifelong learning ensures that investors remain adaptive to evolving market conditions and are better equipped to make prudent investment choices.

In summary, investing in the stock market is not a get-rich-quick scheme but a journey that demands diligence, education, and resilience. By adhering to a well-thought-out investment strategy, diversifying intelligently, managing risks effectively, and committing to ongoing learning, investors can position themselves for long-term success in the dynamic world of stocks. Remember, the stock market is a tool for wealth creation, and with careful consideration and strategic planning, it can be a powerful means to achieve financial goals over time.